BELWIN MASTER 1

SAXOPHONE INTERMEDIATE

GRADED SOLOS for the Developing Musician
Composed or Arranged by KEITH SNELL

Volume 2

C000152511

CONTENTS

Design: Odalis Soto

ORIENTATION

This book is the second of three folios of saxophone duets in the Belwin Master Duets, Volume 2, series. As with the Belwin Master Duets, Volume 1, each of these folios contains a collection of graded duets that should prove to be a useful resource for both the student and the teacher of the saxophone.

Each folio contains transcriptions of works from all periods of music history, arrangements of folk songs and traditional tunes, plus a selection of original compositions by the editor. These duets will provide the intermediate with limited challenge in rhythm, range, and key signatures in music that is both instructive and enjoyable to perform. The teacher will find these duets useful because each has been carefully arranged to develop the student's overall instrumental technique and musicianship.

INTERMEDIATE LEVEL - DUETS

The duets in this folio will challenge the advancing, intermediate saxophone student in all areas of playing technique, as well as provide an increased exposure to more complex rhythms, key signatures and meters. Special emphasis has been placed on exposing the student to a wide range of musical styles from all periods of history. It is hoped that these saxophone duets will provide new challenges to the advancing student while encouraging a broader interest in the many styles of music.

Fughetta

Johann Pachelbel (1653-1706)

Allegretto

Joseph Haydn (1732-1809)

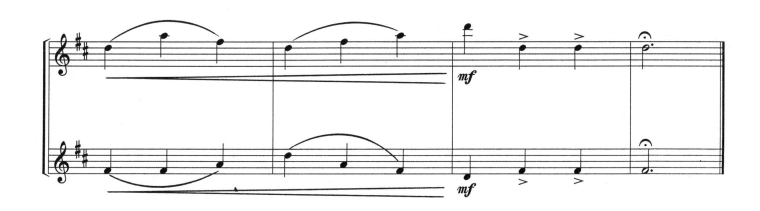

Down By The Riverside

American Negro Spiritual

Gigue

George Frideric Handel (1685-1759)

Menuett

Wilhelm Friedemann Bach (1710-1784)

March for Little John

Keith Snell

Bourrée

from the French Suite, No. 5, BWV 816

Johann Sebastian Bach (1685-1750)

Gavotte

George Frideric Handel (1685-1759)

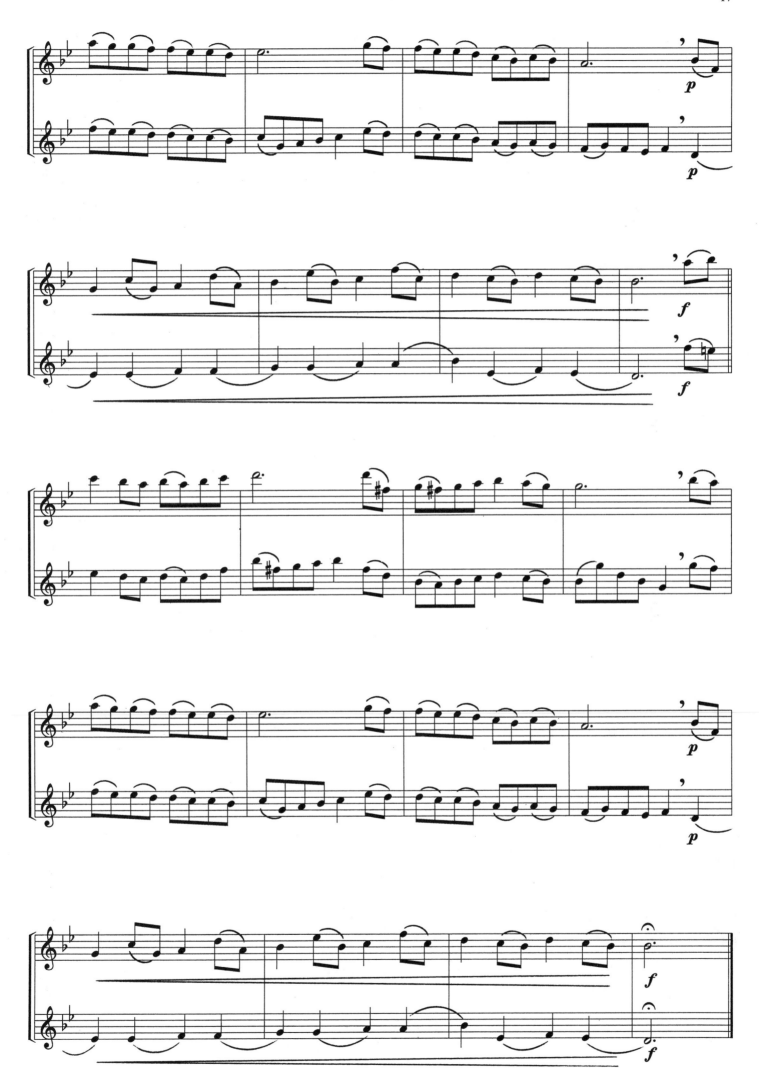

Sonatina

Johann Gottfried Reiche (1667-1734)

Brightly

Folk Dance

Danish Traditional

Windmills

Keith Snell

Sonatina

Jakob Schmitt (c. 1750)

Round

William Byrd (1542-1623)

Rondo

from Sonate Op. 39, No. 2

Muzio Clementi (1752-1832)

Etude

Charles Gounod (1818-1893)